Wake Up, Woods

For Rachel and Soren
and all children who find delight in the awakening woods

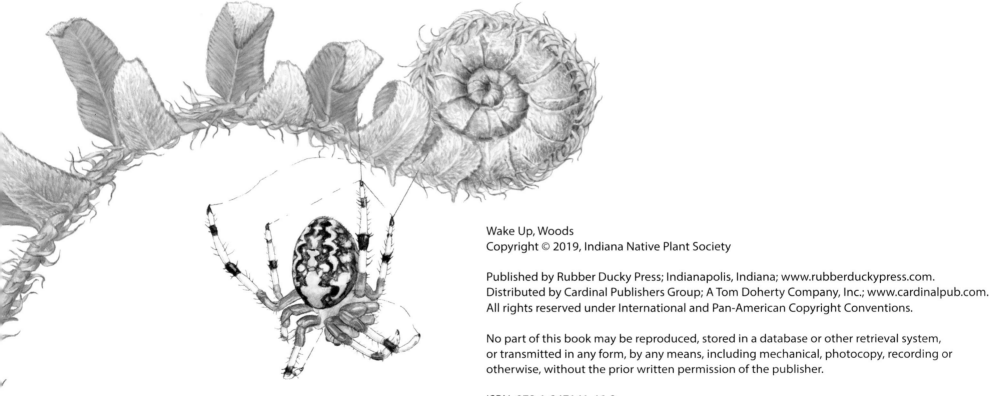

Wake Up, Woods
Copyright © 2019, Indiana Native Plant Society

Published by Rubber Ducky Press; Indianapolis, Indiana; www.rubberduckypress.com.
Distributed by Cardinal Publishers Group; A Tom Doherty Company, Inc.; www.cardinalpub.com.

ISBN: 978-1-947141-46-9

Book Design: Patricia Prather
Illustrator: Gillian Harris
Text: Michael Homoya
Verses: Shane Gibson

Printed in Canada
10 9 8 7 6 5 4 3 2   21 22 23 24 25 26 27 28

Wake Up, Woods

ILLUSTRATIONS Gillian Harris | TEXT Michael Homoya | VERSES Shane Gibson

RUBBER DUCKY PRESS | INDIANAPOLIS, INDIANA

Bloodroot

Sanguinaria canadensis

Bloodroot red
Quick flash of white
Up this morning
Gone tonight

WINNOW ANT

Named for its blood-colored sap, bloodroot plants arise from the ground in early spring before leaves emerge in the trees above. These plants, like true spring ephemerals, take in the sun's vital rays while they can and store energy for the next year's growth. Small native bees pollinate bloodroot flowers, but they don't have much time because each plant's flower is short lived, often lasting only a day or two. After bloodroot goes to seed, elaiosomes (food bodies) that are attached to the seeds attract ants, which carry the seeds to their nests underground. Some ants carry them as far as forty feet away from the plant! The ants eat the food bodies, leaving the seeds underground to germinate and grow into new plants.

MINING BEE

FALSE BLISTER BEETLES

Trout lilies

Erythronium americanum and E. albidum

Dappled sun, mottled leaves
A solitary flower
A ray of hope for ants and bees
In an April shower

FIELD ANT

Yellow and white trout lilies are common early-spring wildflowers that are nearly identical except for their color. They look like a lily you might find in a flower shop, just much smaller. Their thick green leaves are normally speckled, like the pattern on the kind of fish called trout. Now you see how it got its name! Sometimes you will find leaves that are solidly green. It's not unusual to see large colonies of trout lily plants with single leaves and no blooms. Watch for plants with two leaves—a sign that they have stored enough energy from the sun to produce a flower. The flowers are visited by a variety of bees, including one called the trout lily mining bee. Like many spring wildflowers, their seeds are dispersed by ants.

METALLIC GREEN
SWEAT BEE

TROUT LILY
MINING BEE

Spring beauty and cutleaf toothwort

Claytonia virginica and Cardamine concatenata

A toothache cure
Radish hot
A root to eat?
Maybe not

WINNOW ANT

WOODLAND VOLE
EATING TOOTHWORT ROOT

Spring beauty and cutleaf toothwort are two of our most common and wide-ranging forest wildflowers. Toothwort ("wort" means plant) is a botanical relative of radish and mustard and may have been named for either the jagged edges of its leaves, the tooth-like appearance of its buried rhizome, or its early use in treating toothaches. Spring beauty's name says it all—it's beautiful and blooms for much of the spring season. At any given site, from the first spring beauty to the last, a period of two months may have passed. The pink stripes of its petals are thought to help direct insects to its nectar. The spring beauty mining bee specializes in gathering the spring beauty's pink-colored pollen for food.

SPRING BEAUTY
MINING BEE

CUCKOO BEE

WEST VIRGINIA WHITE

SMALL SWEAT BEE

WEST VIRGINIA WHITE CATERPILLAR

Violets

Viola family

Fritillary host
Or cupcake topping
Yellow, white, and purple
Color popping

Violet. Is it a name for a plant or a color? It's both, of course, but the plant name came first! However, flowers of violets can also be yellow, cream or white. Violets' distinctive flowers have two upper petals, two side petals and one lower petal. Most are striped at their bases and some have hairy beards! Bees are the primary pollinators of violets, and the violet mining bee specializes in pollinating violets. A kind of butterfly known as a fritillary normally does not pollinate violets, but its caterpillars feed on their leaves. With few exceptions, if there are no violets, there will be no fritillaries. When the plant's seed capsule is ripe and ready, it explodes, forcibly rocketing away the seeds to the ground where they can be dispersed by ants.

GREAT SPANGLED FRITILLARY

VIOLET MINING BEE

SMALL CARPENTER BEE

GREAT SPANGLED FRITILLARY CATERPILLAR

Dutchman's breeches and squirrel corn

Dicentra cucullaria and D. canadensis

When I dream a springtime dream
And make my springtime wishes
A wood thrush sings "ee-oh-lay" and bees buzz
Amongst squirrel corn and Dutchman's breeches

QUEEN BUMBLEBEE

Dutchman's breeches and squirrel corn are closely related. Their foliage and the way the flowers are arranged are so similar they can be confused with one another. But look closely at the flowers and the difference is clear. Spreading spurs of Dutchman's breeches look like pants dangling from a clothes line. The spurs of squirrel corn are rounded—and the blossoms are fragrant. Underground, squirrel corn has small yellow bulblets that look like corn kernels; Dutchman's breeches have pink bulblets. Native bees frequently visit their flowers and seeds get dispersed by ants that feed on the seeds' food bodies.

WINNOW ANT

MASON BEE

FLOWER CRAB SPIDER

Virginia bluebells

Mertensia virginica

Bottomland of blue
Sure looks delicious
For a nectar-loving bee
With a long proboscis

HUMMINGBIRD CLEARWING MOTH

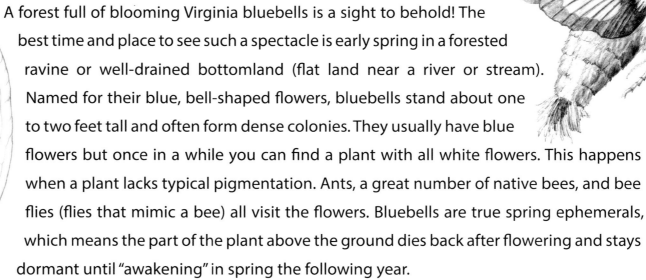

GRAY TREEFROG
ON BLUEBELL LEAF

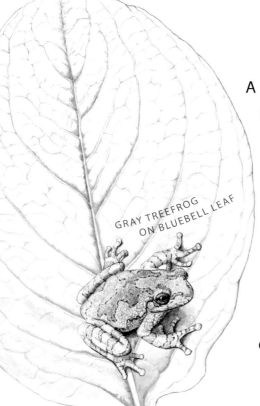

A forest full of blooming Virginia bluebells is a sight to behold! The best time and place to see such a spectacle is early spring in a forested ravine or well-drained bottomland (flat land near a river or stream). Named for their blue, bell-shaped flowers, bluebells stand about one to two feet tall and often form dense colonies. They usually have blue flowers but once in a while you can find a plant with all white flowers. This happens when a plant lacks typical pigmentation. Ants, a great number of native bees, and bee flies (flies that mimic a bee) all visit the flowers. Bluebells are true spring ephemerals, which means the part of the plant above the ground dies back after flowering and stays dormant until "awakening" in spring the following year.

GREATER BEE-FLY

PROBOSCIS

QUEEN BUMBLEBEE

Wood poppy

Stylophorum diphyllum

Yellow-orange sap
Native American dye
Few are as lovely
As our native celandine

When wood poppies are in bloom, it's like having little bursts of sunshine arising from the forest floor. This beautiful wildflower, called either wood poppy or celandine poppy, inhabits rich, moist forests, especially on slopes and in ravines. Wood poppy plants typically grow in single clumps, not in large colonies like some other spring wildflowers. As with violets and other woodland plants, its seeds have food bodies (elaiosomes) that attract animals, especially ants, to help spread seeds out into the forest. Take care not to confuse it with a similar looking relative called greater celandine, which is a non-native invasive weed in natural areas and has flowers smaller than our native wood poppy. Lesser celandine, another invasive weed, has more than four petals and doesn't look like wood poppy.

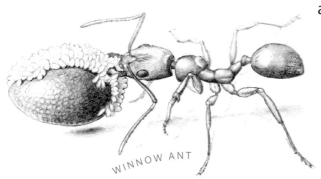

WINNOW ANT

METALLIC GREEN
SWEAT BEE

HOVER FLY

MINING BEE

WHITE-FOOTED MOUSE

Trilliums

Trillium recurvatum and T. grandiflorum

Petals, sepals
And a whorl of leaves
Easy as counting
One, two, three

YELLOW JACKET DISPERSING SEED

Tri means three. When you think of trilliums, think the number three. They support a whorl of three leaves and a single flower with three sepals and three petals. In eastern North America, there are over 25 species of trilliums, with flowers having petals that may be red, purple, pink, white, yellow, or green. Trilliums have two types of flowers. In some species, the flower is attached to a long stalk. In others, the flower totally lacks a stalk. Insects—including bees, wasps, and gnats—are the main pollinators of trilliums. Ants, mice, wasps, and white-tailed deer eat the fruit and disperse the seeds.

REDDISH CARPENTER ANT

GREEN BOTTLE CARRION FLY

MINING BEE

QUEEN BUMBLEBEE

RUNNING CRAB SPIDER

LONG-HORNED FLOWER BEETLE

Mayapple
Podophyllum peltatum

Beneath the umbrella
Of a mayapple's leaf
Hides something tasty
A box turtle's treat

RACCOON

Mayapple is one of the forest's most easily recognized plants because they have large leaves shaped like umbrellas. Mayapples grow in colonies of mostly single-leaved, non-blooming plants. In May, or even earlier, double leaves invite you to bend way over and look for a single white flower with a yellow center hiding beneath the "umbrella." Though they produce little to no nectar, bees and bumblebees do investigate, and the bees spread pollen among the flowers. Its fruit ripens in summer to look like a small yellow apple. White-tailed deer, raccoons, and box turtles eat the "apple" and spread the seeds.

MOREL MUSHROOM

EUROPEAN HONEYBEE

EASTERN BOX TURTLE

Jack-in-the-pulpit and green dragon

Arisaema triphyllum and A. dracontium

In warming woods
Growing tropical and tall
Bearing bundles of red berries
That gleam in summer and fall

WILD TURKEY

Jack-in-the-pulpit and green dragon belong to the Arum family, a diverse group of mostly tropical plants with unusual flower structures. In Jack-in-the-pulpit and green dragon, there is a tube called a spathe that encloses the club-like spadix. The spathes hide tiny flowers that cluster around the base of the spadix. Fungus gnats are common pollinators. The spadix is the "Jack" of Jack-in-the-pulpit, and the whip-like "tongue" of green dragon. "Jack" is often compared to a preacher in a pulpit. Green dragon, with its long protruding tongue and widely fanned leaves brings to mind a mythical dragon. In late summer and fall, both plants call attention to their clusters of bright red berries. Some birds and mammals are known to eat them, but they are poisonous for people to eat.

FUNGUS GNAT

FUNGUS GNAT
AND SPATHE INTERIOR

FUNGUS GNAT

Wild columbine and fire pink

Aquilegia canadensis and Silene virginica

Columbine
And fire pink
For hummingbirds' travels
An essential drink

Very few woodland wildflowers are red, but there are two splendid ones: fire pink and wild columbine. Fire pink, a member of the carnation family, has red flowers that stand out vividly among the white, yellow, and purple hues found in most forest wildflowers. Wild columbine is also ablaze with color, but not with the same intensity as fire pink. It is mostly scarlet, but when combined with its inner circle of yellow petals, it can appear orange from a distance. Look for both in well-drained forest soils, especially on slopes and rocky outcrops. These two native wildflowers are visited and pollinated by ruby-throated hummingbirds, which drink from the deeply hidden reserves of nectar at the tips of the columbine spurs and the base of the tubular fire pink flowers.

COLUMBINE DUSKYWING

MALE RUBY-THROATED HUMMINGBIRD

COLUMBINE DUSKYWING CATERPILLAR

Christmas fern

Polystichum acrostichoides

A fiddlehead
No strings attached
Unfurled beauty
Spring's here at last

WHITE-LIPPED SNAIL

Christmas ferns, like all ferns, have no flowers or seeds. They produce spores instead. While spores are not seeds, they have a similar purpose and are most commonly found on the undersurface of the fern leaf. A germinating spore will grow into a tiny, usually flat and green plant called a gametophyte. It is here where reproductive cells bond together and grow into a new spore-producing fern. In spring, each fern stalk emerges as a curled up "fiddlehead" that slowly unrolls and expands to its full leafy form. Christmas fern's evergreen leaves were once popular for decorating during the Christmas season, thus the common name.

SPRING PEEPER

MARBLED ORB WEAVER

GAMETOPHYTE

Glossary

colony—a group of the same kind of plant living together in the same area

disperse—to spread seeds or spores to a new location

elaiosomes—food bodies rich in lipids (fats) and proteins that are attached to many plant seeds

ephemeral—something that lasts for a short time

fertilization—the union of male and female reproductive cells that leads to the formation of seeds (or in ferns, growth of a new fern plant)

foliage—the leaves of a plant

fragrant—having a strong scent

gametophyte—in ferns, tiny plant tissue upon which reproductive cells may bond together and grow into a plant

germinate—to begin to grow a new plant from a seed or a spore

habitat—a place where a plant or animal lives and thrives

inhabit—to live in a certain place

invasive species—a plant (or animal) that comes to live in a new habitat where it did not previously live and thrives in its new home; they thrive so well that it causes harm to native species

native plant—a plant that has naturally lived in a location for many years and adapted to living in balance with other species in that location; plants introduced by humans from a different continent or region are not considered native

nectar—a sugary fluid produced by flowers that is a food source for many insects and animals; honeybees use nectar to make honey

pigmentation—the natural coloring of a living thing

pollen—a usually yellow powder produced by male plant parts; when this powder is transferred to a female plant part, it will fertilize it so that a seed can be produced; some insects such as bees collect the pollen for food

pollination—when pollen is transferred from a male plant part (anther) to a female plant part (stigma); this enables fertilization to take place

proboscis—a long tube-like mouthpart of an insect

rhizome—an underground stem that grows out from an established plant and sends up new shoots

sap—a fluid containing nutrients that flows through the plant

sepal—a modified leaf around a flower blossom that usually is green like a leaf but sometimes shares the same color as the petal

spadix—a spike of tiny flowers enclosed in a spathe

spathe—a leafy plant part that surrounds a spadix

species—a group of plants (or animals) that have very similar characteristics and can reproduce to make more plants (or animals) of the same kind

spurs—a tube or sac that grows out from the flower; it is often hollow and contains nectar

whorl—an arrangement of leaves in a circle around the same point on the stem

Appendix *Featured species*

Bloodroot
Mining bee *Andrena sp.*
False blister beetles *Asclera ruficollis*
Winnow ant *Aphaenogaster rudis*

Trout lily
Metallic green sweat bee *Augochlorella sp.*
Trout lily mining bee *Andrena erythronii*
Field ant genus *Formica*

Spring beauty and cutleaf toothwort
Woodland vole eating toothwort root *Microtus pinetorum*
Cuckoo bee *Nomada sp.*
Spring beauty mining bee *Andrena erigeniae*
West Virginia white *Pieris virginiensis*
West Virginia white caterpillar *Pieris virginiensis*
Small sweat bee *Lasioglossum sp.*
Winnow ant *Aphaenogaster rudis*

Violet
Upper left, then clockwise:
Bird's foot violet *Viola pedata*
Yellow violet *Viola pubescens*
Common blue violet *Viola sororia*
Spurred violet *Viola rostrata*
Canada violet *Viola canadensis*
Violet mining bee *Andrena violae*

Great spangled fritillary
   Speyeria cybele cybele
Great spangled fritillary
   caterpillar *Speyeria cybele cybele*
Small carpenter bee
   Ceratina sp.

Dutchman's breeches and squirrel corn
Queen bumblebee *Bombus sp.*
Mason bee *Osmia sp.*
Flower crab spider *Misumena vatia*
Winnow ant *Aphaenogaster rudis*

Virginia bluebells
Gray treefrog on bluebell leaf *Hyla sp.*
Hummingbird clearwing moth
   Hemaris thysbe
Greater bee-fly *Bombylius major*
Queen bumblebee *Bombus sp.*

Wood poppy
White-footed mouse *Peromyscus leucopus*
Metallic green sweat bee *Augochlorella sp.*
Hover fly *Family Syrphidae*
Mining bee *Andrena sp.*
Winnow ant *Aphaenogaster rudis*

HUMMINGBIRD CLEARWING MOTH

Christmas fern
White-lipped snail *Neohelix sp.*
Marbled orb weaver *Araneus marmoreus*
Spring peeper *Pseudacris crucifer*

Trillium
Yellow jacket dispersing seed *Vespula maculifrons*
Green bottle carrion fly *Lucilia sp.*
Queen bumblebee *Bombus sp.*
Long-horned flower beetle *Evodinus monticola*
Mining bee *Andrena sp.*
Running crab spider *Mecaphesa asperata*
Reddish carpenter ant *Camponatus castaneus*

Mayapple
Raccoon *Procyon lotor*
Morel mushroom *Morchella sp.*
European honeybee *Apis mellifera*
Eastern box turtle *Terrapene carolina*

Jack-in-the-pulpit and green dragon
Wild turkey *Meleagris gallopavo*
Fungus gnats *Sciaridae spp.*

Wild columbine and fire pink
Columbine duskywing, tiny and rare *Erynnis horatius*
Columbine duskywing caterpillar *Erynnis lucilius*
Male ruby-throated hummingbird *Archilochus colubris*

Appendix
Eastern chipmunk *Tamias striatus*

Contributors
Six-spotted tiger beetle *Cicindela sexguttata*
Luna moth *Actias luna*
Cerulean warbler *Setophaga cerulea*
Gray treefrog *Hyla sp.*

Thank You
Red eft (juvenile terrestrial stage of the aquatic
    Eastern Newt) *Notophthalmus viridescens*
Scarlet elf cup fungus *Sarcoscypha sp.*

EASTERN CHIPMUNK

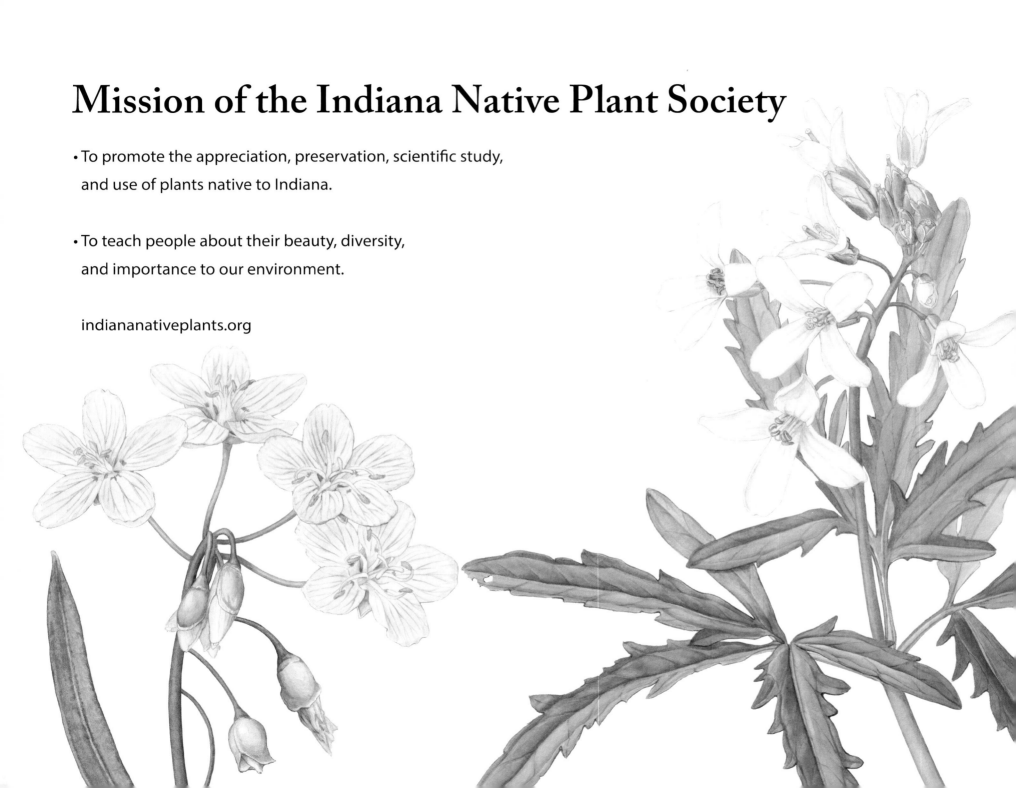

Mission of the Indiana Native Plant Society

• To promote the appreciation, preservation, scientific study,
  and use of plants native to Indiana.

• To teach people about their beauty, diversity,
  and importance to our environment.

indiananativeplants.org

Where to find these native wildflowers

The species in this book range far and wide in much of eastern North America's deciduous forests and even into parts of eastern Canada.

Many cities and counties maintain woodlands that showcase native plants in the spring. Check shady, unmowed sections in parks and undeveloped areas that you visit. Look for them in federal and state forests, nature preserves and properties protected by organizations such as regional land trusts. You may even find them in shady gardens in your neighborhood where native plants are nurtured to benefit wildlife and to give us year-round pleasure.

This book offers a glimpse into the forest life that thrives in the springtime, but it cannot illustrate and define all of it. There are many helpful guides and websites too numerous to list here. Native plant societies, present in many states, provide a wealth of information as well.

Contributors

ILLUSTRATOR

As a natural history illustrator and botanical artist, Gillian Harris works at the intersection of art and science. Gillian has studied at Indiana University, Harvard University, and the University of Michigan. She has illustrated field guides and garden books, and has exhibited her illustrations in zoos, botanical gardens, and at the Smithsonian National Museum of Natural History. Gillian loves to hike; one of her favorite places is the Great Smoky Mountains. She also draws inspiration from the wild plants and animals she encounters in the Great Lakes region and in her own backyard, the wooded uplands of southern Indiana.

LUNA MOTH

BOTANIST AND ECOLOGIST

Michael Homoya was a botanist and plant ecologist for the Indiana Department of Natural Resources Natural Heritage Program for 37 years prior to his retirement in 2019. Mike discovered, inventoried, and assessed natural communities to determine what should be included as state dedicated nature preserves. He also monitored rare species to update the official Indiana list of rare, threatened, and endangered vascular plants. He has shared his knowledge, experience, and enthusiasm about plants by authoring several books, teaching at the collegiate level, and serving as president of professional science associations. In keeping with his passion for plants, his motto is: "Always Be Botanizing!"

SIX-SPOTTED TIGER BEETLE

POET

At an early age, Shane Gibson's dad immersed him in nature through fishing, hunting, searching for morel mushrooms, walking the farm for historical artifacts, and just playing outside. This immersion in nature grew into a life-long passion for the outdoors. With degrees in environmental science and elementary education from Indiana University, Shane enjoys blending his love of the outdoors, writing, and literature. He is Environmental Education Director for Sycamore Land Trust and has worked as a teacher and naturalist. Shane has envisioned his poetry in book form for many years and is thankful for this publication. Shane lives in Monroe County, Indiana, with his wife Taji, two boys Tanner and Sawyer, and a slew of flea-bitten varmints.

CERULEAN WARBLER

GRAY TREE FROG

***WAKE UP, WOODS* COMMITTEE**

Indiana Native Plant Society members Ruth Ann Ingraham, Melissa Moran, and Carolyn Wamsley volunteered to bring Wake Up, Woods to fruition, driven by an appreciation for our natural world and a desire to help the next generation enjoy exploring the world around us.

Thank you!

Organizations and individuals shared the excitement of creating a children's book about native woodland plants by donating funds to make it happen. Through their generosity, readers young and old will be able to learn about spring's woodland awakening and share their discoveries and amazement with others.

RED EFT

Indiana Native Plant Society

The Nature Conservancy

Indiana Academy of Science

Central Indiana Land Trust

Niches Land Trust

Reconnecting to Our Waterways and Central Indiana Community Foundation

Sycamore Land Trust

Mark M. Holeman Inc.

— *plus* —

126 friends of nature and children's literature

SCARLET ELF CUP FUNGUS